40 Reproducible Forms
for the Writing Traits Classroom

Checklists, Graphic Organizers, Rubrics and Scoring Sheets, and More to Boost Students' Writing Skills in All Seven Traits

by Ruth Culham & Amanda Wheeler

NEW YORK • TORONTO • LONDON • AUCKLAND • SYDNEY
MEXICO CITY • NEW DELHI • HONG KONG • BUENOS AIRES

■SCHOLASTIC
Teaching
Resources

DEDICATION

*To all the people who support us every day
at The Writing Traits Company*

ACKNOWLEDGMENT

With vision, resolve, and great humor, wonder-editor Ray Coutu is an inspiration from concept to publication. His wisdom and contributions have added to this book in countless ways. As an editor who takes the time to learn the work, he listens to our ideas and makes suggestions to make the text better. It's a talent to be admired, celebrated, and appreciated. Thank you, Ray.

Cover design by Maria Lilja
Interior design by Holly Grundon

Interior photographs: Page 4 and 8 Tom Hurst via SODA; Page 43 Photodisc via SODA

ISBN 0-439-55684-8
Copyright © 2003 by The Writing Traits Company
All rights reserved. Published by Scholastic Inc.
Printed in the U.S.A.

11 12   40   09 08 07 06

Contents

Introduction

"I really love using the traits to teach writing, but now that students are writing so much more and so much better, I'm not sure how to manage it all. Help!" We hear comments like this all the time from teachers across the country...and we've listened.

This book contains forty essential forms to support you and your students in the writing traits classroom. It's divided into two parts: Teaching the Writing Traits and Teaching the Writing Modes. Both parts contain clear guidelines on how and when to use the forms.

The first part has rubrics and scoring sheets to assess student work according to all seven writing traits, a parent letter and ideas for bringing writing into the home, checklists for students to use during revision and editing, and planning and record-keeping forms to assist you in documenting student progress.

The second part focuses on the modes of writing: narrative, expository, persuasive, descriptive, and imaginative. It includes resources for communicating with parents about the modes, checklists to ensure quality writing in the modes, and user-friendly graphic organizers to help students organize and develop their thoughts.

The book can be used on its own or as a companion to *The 6+1 Traits of Writing: The Complete Guide, Grades 3 and Up* (Scholastic, 2003). Since all the forms are full-sized black-line masters, photocopying them and using them with individual students or groups is a breeze.

Some Background on the Traits and Modes of Writing

The traits of writing drive classroom talk. They provide the language we use to describe what writers really do as they draft, revise, and edit. The traits are:

- Ideas: the meaning and development of the message

- Organization: the internal structure of the piece

- Voice: the way the writer brings the topic to life

- Word Choice: the specific vocabulary the writer uses to convey meaning

- Sentence Fluency: the way the words and phrases flow throughout the text

- Conventions: the mechanical correctness of the piece

- Presentation: the overall appearance of the work

Using the rubrics and scoring sheets on pages 11–19, a teacher—perhaps together with a student—assesses a piece of writing for all traits, identifies a trait or traits to work on, and looks for ways to revise. A student may need a better introduction (organization). A place in the writing may not make sense and needs clarifying (ideas). Maybe a student is struggling to find the right word or phrase to bring an idea to life (word choice). The piece may read smoothly in some parts and awkwardly in others (sentence fluency). There may be spots in the writing where the reader doesn't connect to what the writer is trying to say (voice). As the piece gets closer to being ready to share, the student needs to make sure the spelling, punctuation, grammar and usage, capitalization, and paragraphing are all in place (conventions). Teachers and students use the traits to fine-tune the writing so the message is as clear as possible.

The traits of writing share a powerful partnership with the modes of writing. While the traits help writers develop their work, the modes give them an overall purpose for their work. The modes are:

- Narrative: to tell a story

- Expository: to inform or explain

- Persuasive: to construct an argument

- Descriptive: to paint a picture with words

- Imaginative: to create a new way of seeing things

During prewriting and early drafting, most writers focus on mode. They decide if they are going to tell a story, explain something, describe something, convince the reader of something, create something completely original, or do a combination of these things. Once this important decision is made, writers can turn to the traits as they draft the text and then revise to clarify the ideas, organize for a sensible flow, use an appropriate voice, select the appropriate vocabulary, build sentences that bring the key points to life, apply correct conventions, and present the work in a reader-friendly way. It is the mode, however, that determines the purpose for the writing. And knowing the purpose for the writing is what helps the writer to use the traits effectively.

The Power of Teaching Traits and Modes Together

The choice of the mode has a tremendous influence on how the writer applies the traits. A story, for example, is organized quite differently than an essay. The voice of a persuasive piece is likely to be much more strident than the voice of a story, which is likely to be more entertaining. Consider this assignment: "Write about something you have learned about the Lewis and Clark expedition." A piece that explains how the Lewis and Clark expedition opened up the American West would be quite different from one that tells the story of Meriwether Lewis's life. A description of the coldest day during the expedition would develop in yet another way. Attention to the purpose of writing influences students as they apply the traits to the writing.

Although traits and modes can be taught individually, students make greater strides when we teach them in unison. Of the teachers we work with, those who work with the traits and modes simultaneously get writing of the highest quality. Students get excited when they learn to replace simple, generic words with the more specific vocabulary of text-based writing. Teachers heave a sigh of relief when students stop demanding, "How long does this have to be?" and instead ask for specific feedback such as, "Do you think I have given enough examples in this part for my idea to be clear?" They nod in approval when students question whether the organization they apply suits the mode they have chosen. They smile when students zero in on a topic and treat it with great skill. Each day brings new rewards as students use the traits and modes to write effectively.

The Language That Works in the Writing Classroom

Teachers across the country and around the world have discovered how effective the traits have been in helping their students work to become good writers. If you walk into a trait classroom, you will find students and teachers actively engaged in writing and revising, having small-group and one-on-one conferences, discussing, and collaborating. This all takes place because teachers and students alike talk to each other with clarity and specificity, using a common language. They use the traits to communicate what is working well in their writing and what still needs work. Listen closely to the talk in a writing traits classroom:

> "Franklin, you've captured a beautiful image of what it was like when your grandfather first met your grandmother. It's powerful. Your precision with the language and use of the metaphor, 'like a small polished stone washed up on the beach, she had a sparkle which separated her from all the rest of the young women lined up to catch the bus,' really help me see this and feel it with you. Your word choice and voice are really strong here."

> "I'm intrigued by your use of the dash here, Anikka. Can you tell me why you used it instead of doing something else, like using a semicolon or making two completely different sentences? What is the effect you were going for as you played around with standard conventions?"

> "What a great idea to turn this piece into description, Henry. It works so much better than when you were trying to write it as an essay. The ideas are much clearer, and the words you've used really create a picture in my mind."

> "When I close my eyes, I can hear the rhythm of your phrases and sentences, Emmitt. Let me read this passage from the middle to you and you try doing the same thing. 'When you think about what really makes us human, it's DNA. Can you imagine how intricate a pattern it must take to create a unique human being— each one slightly different or hugely different from the next?' Could you hear how the sentences flow? That part really works for me."

> "Mordiana, how on earth did you ever think to compare an elephant to a skyscraper? It's that kind of original thinking that makes your ideas your own and helps the reader really understand what you are trying to say."

Organizing materials, providing quick and effective feedback, and keeping accurate records is a big part of a writing teacher's reality. This book is designed to lend you a helping hand. We hope it makes your work with students more efficient, more productive, and more gratifying.

—Ruth Culham and Amanda Wheeler

PART I

Reproducible Forms for Teaching the Writing Traits

The writing traits classroom is an exciting and busy place where students, teachers, parents, and administrators use a common vocabulary to support the seven key qualities that define strong writing: ideas (the meaning and development of the message), organization (the internal structure of the piece), voice (the way the writer brings the topic to life), word choice (the specific vocabulary the writer uses to convey meaning), sentence fluency (the way the words and phrases flow throughout the text), conventions (the mechanical correctness of the piece), and presentation (the overall appearance of the work). By using this common vocabulary consistently, you build a solid foundation in what good writing looks like and help all students create it on their own.

The forms in this section support the writing traits classroom. You'll find useful rubrics and scoring sheets for assessing student work, send-home letters that educate and involve parents, checklists to keep students focused, and planning and record-keeping forms to help you get organized and document student work. And because these forms were written using the trait vocabulary consistently, they support one another in a multitude of ways.

Scoring Rubrics and Scoring Sheets

For assessment to be instructive, it must mirror what good writing looks like. In other words, it must make students aware of the criteria for good writing. That way, they can recognize the presence or absence of those criteria in their own work and revise accordingly. The rubrics and scoring sheets in this section help you build that awareness. The rubrics define the criteria for each level of writing development, trait by trait, from "experimenting" to "strong." The corresponding scoring sheets help you assess student writing according to those criteria.

SCORING RUBRICS

The Scoring Rubrics* are quick, easy-to-use references. By defining what good writing looks like in each of the traits, they give you the information you need to score student writing on many levels, to show students how to get from "here" to "there" in conferences, and to communicate with parents. We have included 4-, 5-, and 6-point rubrics. Use the one that best meets your needs.

*Adapted from the five-point scoring guide in *The 6+1 Traits of Writing: The Complete Guide* by Ruth Culham, (Scholastic Inc., 2003). For in-depth writing assessment, refer to that book's full scoring guide for each trait.

SCORING SHEETS

The Scoring Sheets give you ample space to record scores for individual pieces of writing and provide constructive comments. By collecting these forms in writing folders or portfolios, students see their progress in applying the traits throughout the year. We have included 4-, 5-, and 6-point scoring sheets. Use the one that corresponds to your chosen rubric.

Although they are designed primarily for teachers, the scoring sheets and rubrics can also be used by students for assessing practice papers or their own writing.

SEE PAGES 11–13

SEE PAGES 14–16

CUT-APART SCORING SHEETS FOR STUDENTS

These scoring sheets are easy to photocopy, cut apart, and use for many assessment purposes. For example, as students finish writing, have them use the sheet to assess their work and discuss their results in a conference. You can also have students use them to assess practice papers, as a part of a classroom writing activity. We find students love to compare and discuss their scoring with classmates. You may also want to fill out the sheets yourself and attach them directly to student papers.

PRACTICE-PAPER SCORING SHEET

To help students learn to assess their own work for the traits, have them use this form to score practice papers. (You can find practice papers in *6+1 Traits of Writing: The Complete Guide* by Ruth Culham.) As a whole class or in small groups, have students read the same paper. Then have each student score the paper for each trait using the Practice-Paper Scoring Sheet, average their scores to determine a single score for the paper, and discuss results with classmates. Before long, the paper's strengths and weaknesses become evident as scoring patterns emerge from the conversation. This form can also be used for students to self-assess their work during the year.

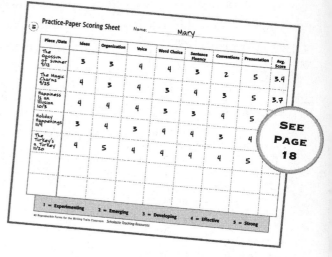

NUMERICAL SCORING SHEET

The Numerical Scoring Sheet is an alternative to the Practice-Paper Scoring Sheet. Rather than filling in scores for each trait, simply circle the appropriate ones and determine an average for the paper.

Four-Point Scoring Rubric

	1 Experimenting	2 Developing	3 Effective	4 Strong
Ideas — the meaning and development of the message	• Searching for a topic • Information limited or missing • No meaningful details • Disconnected thoughts	• Beginning to define topic • Lacks specific information • Vague details • Glimmer of main point	• Topic defined but broad • Content clear but reader still left with questions • Detail support attempted • Begins to develop theme	• Narrow and manageable topic • Goes beyond the obvious or predictable • Relevant, accurate details • Shows connections/insights
Organization — the internal structure of the piece	• No lead or conclusion • Sequencing and pacing not present • Connections are confusing or not present • Hard to follow	• Ineffective lead and conclusion • Sequencing and pacing confusing • Connections awkward • Formulaic structure detracts from content	• Routine lead and conclusion • Mostly logical sequencing and pacing • Predictable connectors • Basic beginning, middle, ending	• Inviting introduction and satisfying conclusion • Effective sequencing and pacing • Thoughtful transitions • Smooth organization
Voice — the way the writer brings the topic to life	• No concern for audience • Lifeless and mechanical • Flat or inappropriate • Purpose not present	• Occasionally intrigues the reader • Generally "risk free" • Sits on the surface • Purpose lacks conviction	• Reader/writer connection present but not strong • Pleasing yet "safe" • Energy level inconsistent • Purpose is credible but not powerful	• Effective and strong reader/writer connection • Takes risks • Reflects interest in and commitment to topic • Purpose is powerful and engaging
Word Choice — the specific vocabulary the writer uses to convey meaning	• Vocabulary is limited • Simple words used incorrectly • No figurative language • Words do not convey meaning	• Generally correct words; no spice • Language is functional • Attempt at figurative language • Words convey general meaning	• Some active verbs and precise nouns • Moments of sparkle here and there • Effective use of figurative language • Words enhance the meaning	• Powerful and engaging words • Wording accurate/specific/precise • Artful use of figurative language • Words/language creates meaningful pictures
Sentence Fluency — the way the words and phrases flow throughout the text	• Choppy, rambling, or incomplete • No "sentence sense" • Oral reading difficult • Repetitive beginnings	• Phrasing effects readability • Sentence structure impairs understanding • Parts invite oral reading • Too many sentences begin the same way	• Sentences more mechanical than fluid • Sentences usually hang together easily • Can be read aloud easily • Sentences begin differently	• Easy flow and rhythm • Strong and varied sentence structure • Invites expressive reading • Overall sentence structure enhances meaning
Conventions — the mechanical correctness of the piece	• Spelling errors impede readability • Incorrect punctuation and capitalization • Many usage and grammar errors • Lack of paragraphing	• Spelling correct on common words • End punctuation and easy capitalization mostly correct • Grammar errors not serious • Paragraphing irregular	• Spelling generally correct • Punctuation and capitalization usually correct • Grammar and usage are correct • Paragraphing correct	• Spelling correct even on more difficult words • Accurate punctuation and capitalization • Grammar and usage contribute to clarity • Paragraphing enhances style
Presentation — the overall appearance of the work	• Handwriting unreadable • Random or lack of spacing • Poor use of white space • Overall appearance is unacceptable	• Handwriting poor • Some thought given to spacing • Attempts at margins and headers • Overall appearance is distracting	• Handwriting mostly legible • Spacing improves clarity • Margins and headers effective • Overall appearance is acceptable	• Handwriting is consistent and uniform • Good balance of space and text • Effectively integrates graphic elements • Overall appearance is pleasing

Five-Point Scoring Rubric

	1 Experimenting	2 Emerging	3 Developing	4 Effective	5 Strong
Ideas — the meaning and development of the message	• Searching for a topic • Limited information • Vague details • Random thoughts	• Hints at topic • Reader left with many unanswered questions • Sporadic details • Glimmer of main point	• General topic defined • Reasonably clear ideas • Details present but not precise • Shows some specifics	• Topic fairly narrowed • New ways of thinking about topic attempted • Credible details with some support • Writer understands topic	• Narrow and manageable topic • Clear, focused, and answers readers' questions • Relevant, accurate details • Shows insight into topic
Organization — the internal structure of the piece	• No lead or conclusion • Sequencing not present • No awareness of pacing • Hard to follow	• Ineffective lead and conclusion • Some sequencing apparent • Pacing awkward • Some attempt at structure	• Routine lead and conclusion • Mainly logical sequencing • Pacing generally under control • Common structures detract from content	• Effective lead and conclusion effective • Sequencing works well • Well-controlled pacing • Smooth flow	• Inviting introduction and satisfying conclusion • Masterful sequencing • Artful pacing used for stylistic effect • Structure showcases the central ideas or theme
Voice — the way the writer brings the topic to life	• No concern for audience • Lifeless and mechanical • Flat or inappropriate • Purpose not present	• Occasionally aware of audience • General statements require reader interpretation • Tries to engage reader • Hints at purpose	• Occasionally intrigues the reader • Pleasing, yet "safe" • Writer/reader connection fades in and out • Purpose inconsistent	• Interesting and informative • Pleasing; takes risks • Engages reader most of the time • Purpose consistent	• Compelling and engaging • Takes effective risks • Reflects interest in and commitment to topic • Purpose is clear and powerful
Word Choice — the specific vocabulary the writer uses to convey meaning	• Vocabulary is limited • Simple words used incorrectly • No figurative language • Words do not convey meaning	• Generally correct words; no spice • Language is functional • Attempts interesting words • Words convey general meaning	• Some active verbs and precise nouns • A moment or two of sparkle • Experiments with figurative language • Words begin to enhance meaning	• Effective and creative verbs and nouns • Wording mostly correct • Figurative language is effective • Words and phrases work well	• Powerful and engaging words • Wording is accurate and precise • Artful use of figurative language • Words/language create meaningful pictures
Sentence Fluency — the way the words and phrases flow throughout the text	• Choppy, rambling, or incomplete • No "sentence sense" • Oral reading not possible • Repetitive beginnings	• Some simple sentences • Occasional connecting word use • Oral reading difficult • Attempts variation in sentence beginnings	• Attempts compound and complex sentences • Sentences usually connect • Parts invite oral reading • Sentences begin in different ways	• Begins to have easy flow and rhythm • Strong and varied structure • Oral reading encourages expression in places • Sentences well crafted	• Polished rhythm, cadence, and flow • Creative use of sentence length and structure • Invites expressive reading • Sentences enhance meaning
Conventions — the mechanical correctness of the piece	• Spelling errors impede readability • Incorrect punctuation and capitalization • Many grammar errors • Lack of paragraphing	• Spelling errors on easy words • Errors on basic punctuation and capitalization • Some usage and grammar errors • Occasional use of paragraphing	• Spelling generally correct on basic words • Routine punctuation and capitalization • Grammar errors infrequent • Consistent paragraphing	• Few spelling errors even on more difficult words • Consistent use of punctuation and capitalization • Grammar and usage correct • Paragraphing stylistically effective	• Spelling correct even on more difficult words • Accurate and creative use of punctuation and capitalization • Grammar and usage contribute to clarity and style • Sound and creative paragraphing
Presentation — the overall appearance of the work	• Handwriting unreadable • Random spacing or lack of spacing • Poor use of white space • Overall appearance unacceptable	• Handwriting poor • Some thought given to spacing • Attempts at margins/headers • Overall appearance is distracting	• Handwriting mostly readable but inconsistent • Attempts consistent spacing • Margins and headers effective • Overall appearance is acceptable	• Legible handwriting • Spacing improves clarity • Experiments with graphic elements • Overall appearance shows balance and proportion	• Consistent and uniform handwriting • Good balance of space and text • Effectively integrates graphic elements • Overall appearance is pleasing

Six-Point Scoring Rubric

	1 Experimenting	2 Emerging	3 Developing	4 Effective	5 Strong	6 Exceptional
Ideas — the meaning and development of the message	• Searching for a topic • Limited information • Vague details • Random thoughts	• Hints at topic • Reader left with many unanswered questions • Sporadic details • Glimmer of main point	• General topic defined • Reasonably clear ideas • Details present but not precise • Shows some specifics	• Topic fairly narrowed • New ways of thinking about topic attempted • Credible details with some support • Writer understands topic	• Narrow and manageable topic • Clear and focused; answers readers' questions • Relevant, accurate details enrich theme • Shows insight into topic	• Unique treatment of topic • In-depth understanding of topic • Unusual details go beyond the obvious • Makes connections; shares insights effectively
Organization — the internal structure of the piece	• No lead or conclusion • Sequencing not present • No awareness of pacing • Hard to follow	• Ineffective lead and conclusion • Some sequencing apparent • Pacing awkward • Some attempt at structure	• Routine lead and conclusion • More logical sequencing • Pacing generally under control • Common structures detract from content	• Effective lead and conclusion • Sequencing works well • Well-controlled pacing • Common structures have smooth flow	• Inviting introduction and satisfying conclusion • Effective sequencing • Pacing is creative • Structure begins to reveal theme	• Introduction and conclusion are unique but connected • Masterful sequencing • Artful pacing used for stylistic effect • Structure showcases central ideas or theme
Voice — the way the writer brings the topic to life	• No concern for audience • Lifeless and mechanical • Flat or inappropriate • Purpose not present	• Occasionally aware of audience • General statements require reader interpretation • Tries to engage • Hints at purpose	• Writer begins to connect with the reader • Pleasing, yet "safe" • Writer/reader connection fades in and out • Purpose inconsistent	• Writer occasionally intrigues the reader • Pleasing; takes risks • Engages reader most of the time • Purpose consistent	• Interesting and informative • Takes effective risks • Reflects interest and commitment in topic • Purpose shows clarity and understanding	• Compelling and engaging • Writer goes out on a limb • Displays ownership of the topic • Powerful purpose shows commitment
Word Choice — the specific vocabulary the writer uses to convey meaning	• Vocabulary is limited • Simple words used incorrectly • No figurative language • Words do not convey meaning	• Generally correct words; no spice • Language is functional • Attempts at interesting words • Words convey general meaning	• Some active verbs and precise nouns • A moment or two of sparkle • Experiments with figurative language • Words begin to enhance meaning	• Effective and creative verbs and nouns • Wording mostly correct • Accurate use of figurative language • Words and phrases work well	• Precision with words and phrases • Wording works effectively • Figurative language is effective • Words and phrases create picture	• Powerful, engaging, and "just-right" words • Wording is accurate and precise • Artful use of figurative language • Words and phrases create lingering images
Sentence Fluency — the way the words and phrases flow throughout the text	• Choppy, rambling, or incomplete • No "sentence sense" • Oral reading is not possible • Repetitive beginnings	• Some simple sentences • Occasional connecting word use • Oral reading difficult • Attempts variation in sentence beginnings	• Attempts compound and complex sentences • Sentences usually connect • Parts invite oral reading • Sentences begin in different ways	• Begins to have easy flow and rhythm • Strong and varied structure • Oral reading encourages expression in places • Sentences well crafted	• Rhythm and flow feel natural • Creative use of sentence length and structure • Invites expressive reading • Sentences relate and build upon one another	• Carefully honed cadences • Exquisitely constructed sentences • Reading aloud is a breeze • Sentences enhance meaning
Conventions — the mechanical correctness of the piece	• Spelling errors impede readability • Incorrect punctuation and capitalization • Many usage and grammar errors • Lack of paragraphing	• Spelling errors even on easy words • Errors on basic punctuation and capitalization • Some usage and grammar errors • Occasional use of paragraphing	• Spelling generally correct or basic words • Routine punctuation and capitalization • Grammar errors infrequent • Consistent paragraphing	• Few spelling errors even on more difficult words • Consistent use of punctuation and capitalization • Grammar and usage correct • Correct use of paragraphing	• Spelling correct even on more difficult words • Accurate use of punctuation and capitalization • Standard grammar and usage are under control • Sound and creative paragraphing	• Uses unique spellings for style • Stylistic use of punctuation/capitalization • Grammar and usage contribute to clarity and style • Paragraphing is stylistically effective
Presentation — the overall appearance of the work	• Handwriting unreadable • Random spacing or lack of spacing • Poor use of white space • Overall appearance unacceptable	• Handwriting poor • Some thought given to spacing • Attempts at margins and headers • Overall appearance distracting	• Handwriting mostly readable but inconsistent • Attempts consistent spacing • Margins and headers effective • Overall appearance is acceptable	• Legible handwriting • Spacing improves clarity • Experiments with graphic elements • Overall appearance shows balance and proportion	• Handwriting is consistent • Good balance of space and text • Effectively integrates graphic elements • Overall appearance makes it easy to read	• Handwriting shows uniform slant, spacing, and letter formation • White space and text work in harmony • Graphic elements and text are synchronized and aligned • Overall appearance is pleasing

Four-Point Scoring Sheet

Name: _____

Date: _____

Piece:	1 Experimenting	2 Developing	3 Effective	4 Strong
Ideas the meaning and development of the message				
Organization the internal structure of the piece				
Voice the way the writer brings the topic to life				
Word Choice the specific vocabulary the writer uses to convey meaning				
Sentence Fluency the way the words and phrases flow throughout the text				
Conventions the mechanical correctness of the piece				
Presentation the overall appearance of the work				

Five-Point Scoring Sheet

Name: _____

Date: _____

Piece:	1 Experimenting	2 Emerging	3 Developing	4 Effective	5 Strong
Ideas the meaning and development of the message					
Organization the internal structure of the piece					
Voice the way the writer brings the topic to life					
Word Choice the specific vocabulary the writer uses to convey meaning					
Sentence Fluency the way the words and phrases flow throughout the text					
Conventions the mechanical correctness of the piece					
Presentation the overall appearance of the work					

Six-Point Scoring Sheet

Name: _____

Date: _____

Piece:	1 Experimenting	2 Emerging	3 Developing	4 Effective	5 Strong	6 Exceptional
Ideas the meaning and development of the message						
Organization the internal structure of the piece						
Voice the way the writer brings the topic to life						
Word Choice the specific vocabulary the writer uses to convey meaning						
Sentence Fluency the way the words and phrases flow throughout the text						
Conventions the mechanical correctness of the piece						
Presentation the overall appearance of the work						

Cut-Apart Scoring Sheets

Piece: _____ Scorer: _____

Trait	1	2	3	4	5
Ideas the meaning and development of the message					
Organization the internal structure of the piece					
Voice the way the writer brings the topic to life					
Word Choice the specific vocabulary the writer uses to convey meaning					
Sentence Fluency the way the words and phrases flow throughout the text					
Conventions the mechanical correctness of the piece					
Presentation the overall appearance of the work					

Write your comments and suggestions on the back of this sheet.

Piece: _____ Scorer: _____

Trait	1	2	3	4	5
Ideas the meaning and development of the message					
Organization the internal structure of the piece					
Voice the way the writer brings the topic to life					
Word Choice the specific vocabulary the writer uses to convey meaning					
Sentence Fluency the way the words and phrases flow throughout the text					
Conventions the mechanical correctness of the piece					
Presentation the overall appearance of the work					

Write your comments and suggestions on the back of this sheet.

Piece: _____ Scorer: _____

Trait	1	2	3	4
Ideas the meaning and development of the message				
Organization the internal structure of the piece				
Voice the way the writer brings the topic to life				
Word Choice the specific vocabulary the writer uses to convey meaning				
Sentence Fluency the way the words and phrases flow throughout the text				
Conventions the mechanical correctness of the piece				
Presentation the overall appearance of the work				

Write your comments and suggestions on the back of this sheet.

Piece: _____ Scorer: _____

Trait	1	2	3	4	5	6
Ideas the meaning and development of the message						
Organization the internal structure of the piece						
Voice the way the writer brings the topic to life						
Word Choice the specific vocabulary the writer uses to convey meaning						
Sentence Fluency the way the words and phrases flow throughout the text						
Conventions the mechanical correctness of the piece						
Presentation the overall appearance of the work						

Write your comments and suggestions on the back of this sheet.

Practice-Paper Scoring Sheet

Name: _____

Piece/Date	Ideas	Organization	Voice	Word Choice	Sentence Fluency	Conventions	Presentation	Avg. Score

1 = Experimenting   2 = Emerging   3 = Developing   4 = Effective   5 = Strong

40 Reproducible Forms for the Writing Traits Classroom *Scholastic Teaching Resources*

Numerical Scoring Sheet

Name: _____

Piece/Date	Ideas	Organization	Voice	Word Choice	Sentence Fluency	Conventions	Presentation	Avg. Score
	1 2 3 4 5	1 2 3 4 5	1 2 3 4 5	1 2 3 4 5	1 2 3 4 5	1 2 3 4 5	1 2 3 4 5	
	1 2 3 4 5	1 2 3 4 5	1 2 3 4 5	1 2 3 4 5	1 2 3 4 5	1 2 3 4 5	1 2 3 4 5	
	1 2 3 4 5	1 2 3 4 5	1 2 3 4 5	1 2 3 4 5	1 2 3 4 5	1 2 3 4 5	1 2 3 4 5	
	1 2 3 4 5	1 2 3 4 5	1 2 3 4 5	1 2 3 4 5	1 2 3 4 5	1 2 3 4 5	1 2 3 4 5	
	1 2 3 4 5	1 2 3 4 5	1 2 3 4 5	1 2 3 4 5	1 2 3 4 5	1 2 3 4 5	1 2 3 4 5	
	1 2 3 4 5	1 2 3 4 5	1 2 3 4 5	1 2 3 4 5	1 2 3 4 5	1 2 3 4 5	1 2 3 4 5	
	1 2 3 4 5	1 2 3 4 5	1 2 3 4 5	1 2 3 4 5	1 2 3 4 5	1 2 3 4 5	1 2 3 4 5	
	1 2 3 4 5	1 2 3 4 5	1 2 3 4 5	1 2 3 4 5	1 2 3 4 5	1 2 3 4 5	1 2 3 4 5	
	1 2 3 4 5	1 2 3 4 5	1 2 3 4 5	1 2 3 4 5	1 2 3 4 5	1 2 3 4 5	1 2 3 4 5	
	1 2 3 4 5	1 2 3 4 5	1 2 3 4 5	1 2 3 4 5	1 2 3 4 5	1 2 3 4 5	1 2 3 4 5	
	1 2 3 4 5	1 2 3 4 5	1 2 3 4 5	1 2 3 4 5	1 2 3 4 5	1 2 3 4 5	1 2 3 4 5	
	1 2 3 4 5	1 2 3 4 5	1 2 3 4 5	1 2 3 4 5	1 2 3 4 5	1 2 3 4 5	1 2 3 4 5	
	1 2 3 4 5	1 2 3 4 5	1 2 3 4 5	1 2 3 4 5	1 2 3 4 5	1 2 3 4 5	1 2 3 4 5	
	1 2 3 4 5	1 2 3 4 5	1 2 3 4 5	1 2 3 4 5	1 2 3 4 5	1 2 3 4 5	1 2 3 4 5	
	1 2 3 4 5	1 2 3 4 5	1 2 3 4 5	1 2 3 4 5	1 2 3 4 5	1 2 3 4 5	1 2 3 4 5	

1 = Experimenting   2 = Emerging   3 = Developing   4 = Effective   5 = Strong

40 Reproducible Forms for the Writing Traits Classroom   *Scholastic Teaching Resources*

Parent Communication

Most parents want to help their children succeed in school, but they are not always sure how. By introducing the language of the traits to them early in the year, and by encouraging parents' help throughout the year, you can open school-to-home communication lines that lead to writing success for students.

PARENT LETTER ON TRAITS

This letter explains to parents what the traits are and how to help children apply them wisely. Whether you sign, photocopy, and send it home as is, or adapt it to meet your individual goals, the letter paves the way to open communication about writing between parent and child, early in the school year.

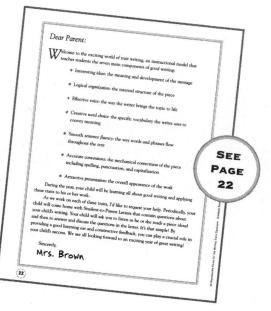

SEE PAGE 22

ACTIVITIES TO ENCOURAGE WRITING AT HOME

These activities provide parents with a host of ways to encourage writing at home. Each activity offers students practice by sparking thinking about one or more of the traits. By photocopying all of the activities to the back of the parent letter, you can supply a useful, one-page menu of options to consider. You might also periodically send home individual activities to keep fresh ideas flowing throughout the year.

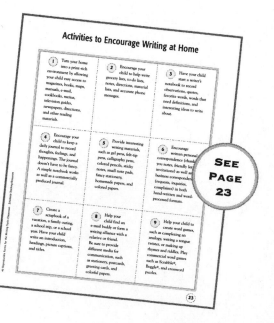

SEE PAGE 23

STUDENT-TO-PARENT LETTERS

The Student-to-Parent Letters invite parents to interact with their children about their writing. As you work on each trait, make photocopies of the appropriate letter, distribute them to students, and have students attach the letter to their writing. At home, students should read their work aloud to a parent and ask the questions in the letter. The answers always spur good dialogue, as well as ideas for editing and revision. Sending these letters home on a regular basis will help parents become more skilled at encouraging improvements.

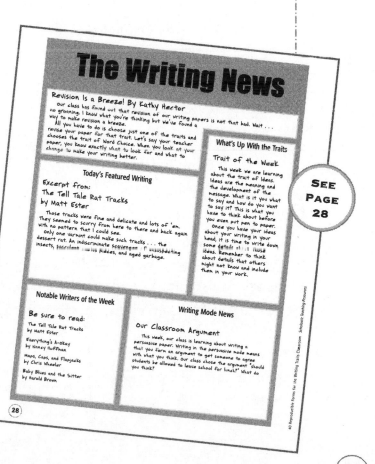

SEE PAGES 24–27

WRITING NEWSLETTER TEMPLATE

Sending out a Writing Newsletter is a great way to keep parents and administrators informed about what is happening in writing class. Have student volunteers write the copy for each block and then, using the template, format the text in one of the following ways:

1. Fill it in by hand.

2. Type it into a word processor, print it out, and paste it into the blocks.

3. Design the whole newsletter on screen and print it out onto a copy of the template.

Deciding who will write each section, who will be in charge of design, and how often the newsletter will be published is a great classroom activity that can become a regular part of your writing curriculum.

SEE PAGE 28

Dear Parent:

Welcome to the exciting world of trait writing, an instructional model that teaches students the seven main components of good writing:

- ◆ Interesting *ideas*: the meaning and development of the message

- ◆ Logical *organization*: the internal structure of the piece

- ◆ Effective *voice*: the way the writer brings the topic to life

- ◆ Creative *word choice*: the specific vocabulary the writer uses to convey meaning

- ◆ Smooth *sentence fluency*: the way words and phrases flow throughout the text

- ◆ Accurate *conventions*: the mechanical correctness of the piece including spelling, punctuation, and capitalization

- ◆ Attractive *presentation*: the overall appearance of the work

During the year, your child will be learning all about good writing and applying these traits to his or her work.

As we work on each of these traits, I'd like to request your help. Periodically, your child will come home with Student-to-Parent Letters that contain questions about your child's writing. Your child will ask you to listen as he or she reads a piece aloud and then to answer and discuss the questions in the letter. It's that simple! By providing a good listening ear and constructive feedback, you can play a crucial role in your child's success. We are all looking forward to an exciting year of great writing!

Sincerely,

40 Reproducible Forms for the Writing Traits Classroom *Scholastic Teaching Resources*

Activities to Encourage Writing at Home

1 Turn your home into a print-rich environment by allowing your child easy access to magazines, books, maps, manuals, e-mail, cookbooks, menus, television guides, newspapers, directions, and other reading materials.

2 Encourage your child to help write grocery lists, to-do lists, notes, directions, material lists, and accurate phone messages.

3 Have your child start a writer's notebook to record observations, quotes, favorite words, words that need definitions, and interesting ideas to write about.

4 Encourage your child to keep a daily journal to record thoughts, feelings, and happenings. The journal doesn't have to be fancy. A simple notebook works as well as a commercially produced journal.

5 Provide interesting writing materials, such as gel pens, felt-tip pens, calligraphy pens, colored pencils, sticky notes, small note pads, fancy stationery, homemade papers, and colored papers.

6 Encourage written personal correspondence (thank you notes, friendly letters, invitations) as well as business correspondence (requests, inquiries, complaints) in both hand-written and word-processed formats.

7 Create a scrapbook of a vacation, a family outing, a school trip, or a school year. Have your child write an introduction, headings, picture captions, and titles.

8 Help your child find an e-mail buddy or form a writing alliance with a relative or friend. Be sure to provide different media for communication, such as stationery, postcards, greeting cards, and colorful papers.

9 Help your child to create word games, such as completing an analogy, writing a tongue twister, or making up rhymes and riddles. Play commercial word games such as Scrabble®, Boggle®, and crossword puzzles.

Dear _____ ,

In writing class, we are working on the trait of **IDEAS** (the meaning and development of the message). Would you help me become a better writer by listening to me read my paper aloud, then answering the following questions?
Thanks,

1. What was the most important thing you learned from my writing?

2. What interesting details did I include that taught you something new?

3. What questions about this topic would you like to have answered in my next draft?

4. Which paragraph do you think best demonstrates my knowledge of this subject?

- -

Dear _____ ,

In writing class, we are working on the trait of **ORGANIZATION** (the internal structure of the piece). Would you help me become a better writer by listening to me read my paper aloud, then answering the following questions?
Thanks,

1. Did the introduction capture your interest and make you want to keep listening?

2. Were there places in my writing where I should have sped up or slowed down? Where?

3. Did I give you something interesting to think about in my conclusion? If so, what?

4. Did the title give you insight into what the writing was going to be about? Why or why not?

40 Reproducible Forms for the Writing Traits Classroom *Scholastic Teaching Resources*

Dear_____ ,

In writing class, we are working on the trait of **VOICE** (the way the writer brings the topic to life). Would you help me become a better writer by listening to me read my paper aloud, then answering the following questions?
Thanks,

1. Does my writing give a clear sense of the person behind the words?

2. What risks do you think I have taken in this piece?

3. Does my point of view come through loud and clear?

4. Do you think my writing is appropriate for my audience? Why? Why not?

Dear_____ ,

In writing class, we are working on the trait of **WORD CHOICE** (the specific vocabulary the writer uses to convey meaning). Would you help me become a better writer by listening to me read my paper aloud, then answering the following questions?
Thanks,

1. Do the words I use make it easy to understand what I mean? What words are unclear?

2. What words or phrases created a picture in your mind?

3. Does the language seem natural? Is it effective in getting the meaning across?

4. Do you think I used the right words in just the right places? Where did I? Where didn't I?

Dear _____ ,

In writing class, we are working on the trait of **SENTENCE FLUENCY** (the way words and phrases flow throughout the text). Would you help me become a better writer by listening to me read my paper aloud, then answering the following questions?

Thanks,

1. Did I vary the beginnings and lengths of my sentences to add energy?

2. Do the connecting words between sentences show how each sentence relates to the one before it?

3. Do you think the writing exhibits a smooth flow of words and phrases that makes it easy for me to read it aloud?

4. Are the sentences constructed in a way that enhances the meaning of the writing?

- -

Dear _____ ,

In writing class, we are working on the trait of **CONVENTIONS** (the mechanical correctness of the piece such as spelling, punctuation, and capitalization). Would you help me become a better writer by reading my paper, then answering the following questions?

Thanks,

1. When reading my paper, do you feel that the punctuation and capitalization are correct? Do you see evidence of any creative punctuation? Where?

2. Did my correct use of grammar lend style and clarity to the writing?

3. Do you feel that I used sound paragraphing to organize my paper?

4. If you could rate the readability of this paper on a scale of 1 (lowest) to 5 (highest), what would you give it?

Dear_____ ,

In writing class, we are working on the trait of **PRESENTATION** (the overall appearance of the work). Would you help me become a better writer by reading my paper, then answering the following questions?
Thanks,

1. Is my handwriting easy to read? Is the slant of the letters consistent and the spacing uniform between the words? If I used a word processor, is the font size consistent and appropriate for the piece?

2. Does the white space on the page allow you to focus on the text, or is it distracting?

3. Have I successfully used headers, page numbers, graphics, or bullets to make it easy to find information?

4. When appropriate, have I effectively integrated charts, graphs, maps, tables, or illustrations into the text?

- -

Dear_____ ,

In writing class, we are working on all of the **traits of writing**. Would you help me become a better writer by listening to me read my paper aloud, reading it yourself, then answering the following questions?
Thanks,

1. Which trait(s) are the strongest in this paper?

| IDEAS | ORGANIZATION | VOICE | WORD CHOICE |
| SENTENCE FLUENCY | CONVENTIONS | PRESENTATION | |

2. If I could work on one trait to improve this piece of writing, which one would it be?

3. If you could rate this paper on a scale of 1 to 5, what score would you give it?
   5 Strong   4 Effective   3 Developing   2 Emerging   1 Experimenting

4. Where do you think my writing has shown the most improvement?

The Writing News

What's Up With the Traits

Today's Featured Writing

Notable Writers of the Week

Writing Mode News

Checklists

Checklists are quick, convenient assessment tools for you and your students. They help you assess how well students understand the traits and can apply them in their writing. Checklists also help students review trait criteria and identify it in their writing.

QUICK CHECKS FOR STUDENTS

These checklists encourage students to review their work for each trait and revise based on what they find. Just make photocopies of the Quick Check for the trait you are working on, hand them out, and have students assess their papers. Once they've finished, assess their papers yourself using the Ready-to-Publish Checklist form on page 37. You might also want to refer to completed Quick Checks in student conferences—they're great for keeping discussions on track.

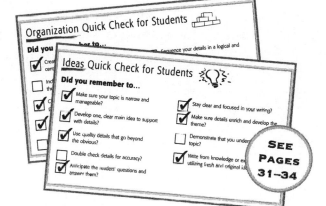

GREAT RATER CHECKLIST

The Great Rater Checklist helps students assess their own papers, practice papers, or classmates' papers fairly. Make photocopies of the checklist, give one to each student, and discuss each section. Then have students score the papers using the rubric of your choice on pages 11–13. Once students have finished, have them read through the Great Rater Checklist, check off appropriate boxes, sign the bottom, and attach it to the scored paper. If students leave any of the boxes unchecked, encourage them to think about why, and then ask them to read and score the writing a second time.

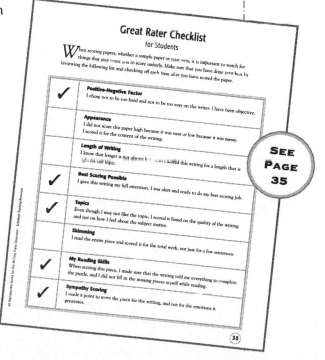

STUDENT PUBLISHING CHECKLISTS

This is a versatile checklist that can be used in its entirety for assessing a paper on all traits, or used in sections for assessing the selected traits. Written in student-friendly language, it allows young writers to hone in on strengths and weaknesses, and to revise purposefully as they take their work to its final stages.

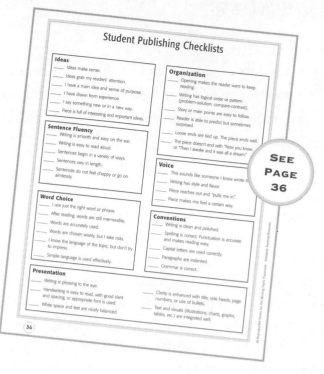

SEE PAGE 36

READY-TO-PUBLISH CHECKLIST

The Ready-to-Publish Checklist is an overall assessment tool for you to use. As students come to you with papers they feel are ready to publish, copy the form, read their papers, and fill in the checklists to show students any areas they need to strengthen. This form corresponds to the Student Quick Checks on pages 31–34. Like the Quick Checks, it can be used in conferences to help students bring their work to a point where it is, in fact, ready to publish.

SEE PAGE 37

Ideas Quick Check for Students

Did you remember to...

☐ Make sure your topic is narrow and manageable?

☐ Develop one, clear main idea to support with details?

☐ Use quality details that go beyond the obvious?

☐ Double check details for accuracy?

☐ Anticipate the readers' questions and answer them?

☐ Stay clear and focused in your writing?

☐ Make sure details enrich and develop the theme?

☐ Demonstrate that you understand your topic?

☐ Write from knowledge or experience utilizing fresh and original ideas?

Organization Quick Check for Students

Did you remember to...

☐ Create an original title that captures the central theme of the piece?

☐ Include an inviting introduction to draw the reader in?

☐ Choose a structure that matches the purpose and audience of the piece?

☐ Make sure the organization flows so smoothly that readers hardly think about it?

☐ Use thoughtful transitions to clearly show how ideas connect?

☐ Sequence your details in a logical and effective manner?

☐ Elaborate with details in the most effective places?

☐ Control the pace by elaborating when it is necessary and moving on when it is not?

☐ Include a satisfying conclusion that leaves readers with a sense of closure and resolution?

Voice Quick Check for Students

Did you remember to...

☐ Speak to readers in a way that is individual, compelling, and engaging?

☐ Take a risk by revealing who you are and what you think?

☐ Add flavor and texture to your writing by using the right tone and expression?

☐ Choose an appropriate voice for the audience who will be reading it?

☐ Write honestly and personally from the heart if it is a narrative piece?

☐ Write to show genuine commitment to the topic if it is a persuasive or an expository piece?

☐ Create your piece to be easily read aloud, shared, and talked about?

☐ Use voice to make readers think about and react to your point of view?

☐ Show control and consistency in your voice throughout the piece?

Word Choice Quick Check for Students

Did you remember to...

☐ Include accurate words that are specific to your topic so your readers understand exactly what you mean?

☐ Use words and phrases to create pictures that linger in your readers' minds?

☐ Use language that is natural and not overdone, with words and phrases that are unique and effective?

☐ Energize your writing with lively verbs, precise nouns, and modifiers to add depth and specificity?

☐ Take care to put just the right word or phrase in just the right spot?

40 Reproducible Forms for the Writing Traits Classroom   Scholastic Teaching Resources

Sentence Fluency Quick Check for Students

Did you remember to...

- ☐ Create an easy flow, rhythm, and cadence with your sentences?

- ☐ Use well-built and strong sentences to invite expressive oral reading?

- ☐ Construct sentences in a way that underscores and enhances the meaning?

- ☐ Vary your sentences in length as well as structure?

- ☐ Use sentence fragments to add style if appropriate?

- ☐ Make sure dialog, if used, sounds natural?

- ☐ Use purposeful and varied sentence beginnings to add variety and energy?

- ☐ Creatively and appropriately use connectives between sentences to show how they relate to each other?

- ☐ Think about the sound of the words as well as the meaning to make reading aloud a breeze?

Conventions Quick Check for Students

Did you remember to...

- ☐ Make sure your spelling is correct on both easy and difficult words?

- ☐ Use accurate and creative punctuation to help guide your readers?

- ☐ Consistently use correct capitalization throughout your writing?

- ☐ Reinforce the organization of your writing with effective paragraphing?

- ☐ Demonstrate clarity and style with correct grammar and word usage?

- ☐ Consider using stylistic effects to make your writing more interesting?

Presentation Quick Check for Students

Did you remember to...

☐ Check your handwriting for consistent slant, clearly formed letters, and uniform spacing?

☐ Choose an appropriate font and font size if using a word processor?

☐ Format your writing so the white space directs the reader to the text?

☐ Use a title, page numbering, and bullets to make it easy for the reader to find desired information?

☐ Effectively display illustrations, charts, graphs, and tables by using clear alignment between text and visuals?

☐ Review your paper for overall neatness and readability?

All Traits Quick Check for Students

Did you remember to...

☐ Choose a main idea that is fresh and new, has a purpose, and makes sense?

☐ Include a good lead, a story that is easy to follow, and a satisfactory conclusion?

☐ Reach out to your readers with style and flavor to "pull them in"?

☐ Choose your words wisely and accurately without trying to impress?

☐ Create sentences that are easy to read aloud and vary in beginnings and length?

☐ Check all of your spelling, punctuation, capitalization, paragraphing, and grammar?

☐ Make sure your writing is pleasing to the eye, with good handwriting or font choice?

Great Rater Checklist
for Students

When scoring papers, whether a sample paper or your own, it is important to watch for things that may cause you to score unfairly. Make sure that you have done your best by reviewing the following list and checking off each item after you have scored the paper.

	Positive-Negative Factor I chose not to be too hard and not to be too easy on the writer. I have been objective.
	Appearance I did not score this paper high because it was neat or low because it was messy. I scored it for the content of the writing.
	Length of Writing I know that longer is not always better, so I scored this writing for a length that is right for the topic.
	Best Scoring Possible I gave this writing my full attention. I was alert and ready to do my best scoring job.
	Topics Even though I may not like the topic, I scored it based on the quality of the writing and not on how I feel about the subject matter.
	Skimming I read the entire piece and scored it for the total work, not just for a few sentences.
	My Reading Skills When scoring this piece, I made sure that the writing told me everything to complete the puzzle, and I did not fill in the missing pieces myself while reading.
	Sympathy Scoring I made a point to score the piece for the writing, and not for the emotions it generates.

Student Publishing Checklists

Ideas

_____ Ideas make sense.

_____ Ideas grab my readers' attention.

_____ I have a main idea and sense of purpose.

_____ I have drawn from experience.

_____ I say something new or in a new way.

_____ Piece is full of interesting and important ideas.

Sentence Fluency

_____ Writing is smooth and easy on the ear.

_____ Writing is easy to read aloud.

_____ Sentences begin in a variety of ways.

_____ Sentences vary in length.

_____ Sentences do not feel choppy or go on aimlessly.

Word Choice

_____ I use just the right word or phrase.

_____ After reading, words are still memorable.

_____ Words are accurately used.

_____ Words are chosen wisely, but I take risks.

_____ I know the language of the topic, but don't try to impress.

_____ Simple language is used effectively.

Organization

_____ Opening makes the reader want to keep reading.

_____ Writing has logical order or pattern (problem-solution, compare-contrast).

_____ Story or main points are easy to follow.

_____ Reader is able to predict but sometimes surprised.

_____ Loose ends are tied up. The piece ends well.

_____ The piece doesn't end with "Now you know…" or "Then I awoke and it was all a dream."

Voice

_____ This sounds like someone I know wrote it.

_____ Writing has style and flavor.

_____ Piece reaches out and "pulls me in."

_____ Piece makes me feel a certain way.

Conventions

_____ Writing is clean and polished.

_____ Spelling is correct. Punctuation is accurate and makes reading easy.

_____ Capital letters are used correctly.

_____ Paragraphs are indented.

_____ Grammar is correct.

Presentation

_____ Writing is pleasing to the eye.

_____ Handwriting is easy to read, with good slant and spacing, or appropriate font is used.

_____ White space and text are nicely balanced.

_____ Clarity is enhanced with title, side heads, page numbers, or use of bullets.

_____ Text and visuals (illustrations, charts, graphs, tables, etc.) are integrated well.

Ready-to-Publish Checklist

Ideas

_____ Topic narrow and manageable
_____ One, clear main idea supported with details
_____ Quality details beyond the obvious
_____ Accurate details
_____ Readers' questions anticipated and answered
_____ Clear and focused
_____ Details enrich and develop theme
_____ Understanding of topic demonstrated
_____ Fresh and original ideas apparent

Organization

_____ Original title that captures the theme
_____ Inviting introduction
_____ Structure matches purpose and audience
_____ Organization flows smoothly
_____ Thoughtful transitions show how ideas connect
_____ Logical and effective sequence of details
_____ Effective placement of details
_____ Controlled pace
_____ Satisfying conclusion

Voice

_____ Writing individual, compelling, and engaging
_____ Risks taken
_____ Flavor and texture apparent
_____ Appropriate voice chosen for audience
_____ Writing honest and personal if narrative piece
_____ Commitment shown if persuasive or expository piece
_____ Voice makes reader think about point of view
_____ Voice control and consistency throughout piece
_____ Strong interaction between reader and writer

Word Choice

_____ Accurate and specific topic words
_____ Words and phrases create pictures

Word Choice (continued)

_____ Individual and effective natural language
_____ Striking words and phrases
_____ Lively and energetic verbs
_____ Precise nouns and modifiers
_____ Effective word and phrase placement
_____ Everyday words used well

Sentence Fluency

_____ Easy flow, rhythm, and cadence
_____ Well-built and strong sentences for easy reading
_____ Sentences underscore and enhance meaning
_____ Sentences vary in length and structure
_____ Sentence fragments used if appropriate
_____ Natural dialog, if used
_____ Purposeful and varied sentence beginnings
_____ Creative and appropriate use of connectives

Conventions

_____ Correct spelling
_____ Accurate and creative punctuation
_____ Consistent correct capitalization
_____ Effective paragraphing
_____ Correct grammar and word usage
_____ Creative use of conventions to enhance meaning

Presentation

_____ Handwriting has consistent slant, clearly formed letters, and uniform spacing
_____ Appropriate font and font size if word processed
_____ White space directs reader to text
_____ Proper use of title, side heads, page numbering, and bullets
_____ Effective illustrations, charts, graphs, and tables
_____ Neat and readable

Planning and Record-Keeping Forms

*T*he forms in this section make planning and record keeping easy. They support the assessment tools already presented—and will help keep you organized all year long.

LITERATURE-BASED LESSON PLANNER

This form allows you to create lesson plans for teaching individual traits using favorite children's books. With spaces for filling in required materials, things to think about beforehand, lesson steps, timeframe, reference pages, trait-book connections, and comments, these plans put everything you need at your fingertips. Just photocopy them, fill in the information for your favorite books, teach the lesson, and save to use year after year.

WEEKLY LESSON PLAN FORM

This form helps you simultaneously think about traits of writing and modes of writing (narrative, expository, persuasive, descriptive, imaginative) while you plan your weekly lessons. There's plenty of space to fill in details for each day of the week. Just photocopy completed forms and clip them together to create a collection of trait-based, mode-specific writing lessons.

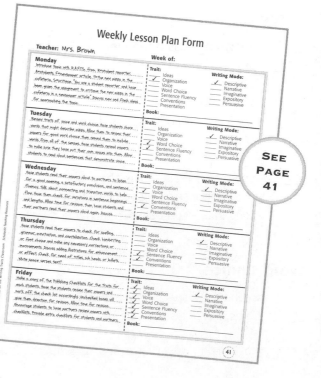

SEE PAGE 40

SEE PAGE 41

YEAR-LONG WRITING ASSESSMENT FORM

Record each student's progress during the year with this form, which contains space for six assessments and a progress chart. Copy a Year-Long Assessment Form for each student and place in his or her writing folder, or keep it with your records. At the beginning of the year, give students a writing assignment, assess the piece using the scoring rubric of your choice on pages 11–13, and record the results on this form. Continue to assess students periodically throughout the year and record results on the same form. To make progress more visible, use a different colored pen or pencil at each assessment period.

SEE PAGE 42

Year-Long Writing Assessment Form

Student Name: **Mary** Grade: **6** Teacher: **Mrs. Brown**

Assessment Date: **9/20** Overall Writing Score 1 ②3 4 5
Assessment Date: **11/15** Overall Writing Score 1 2 ③ 4 5
Assessment Date: **1/25** Overall Writing Score 1 2 ③ 4 5
Assessment Date: **3/12** Overall Writing Score 1 2 3 ④+ 5
Assessment Date: Overall Writing Score 1 2 3 4 5
Assessment Date: Overall Writing Score 1 2 3 4 5

	1 Experimenting	2 Emerging	3 Developing	4 Effective
Ideas	9/20	11/15	1/25	3/12
Organization		9/20	11/15 1/25	3/12
Voice	9/20	11/15	1/25	3/12
Word Choice		9/20	11/15 1/25	3/12
Sentence Fluency		9/20	11/15 1/25	3/12
Conventions		9/20	11/15 1/25	3/12
Presentation	9/20	11/15	9/20 1/25	11/15 1/25 3/12

40 Reproducible Forms for the Writing Traits Classroom Scholastic Teaching Resources

Literature-Based Lesson Planner

Teacher: .... Date: ....

Book Title: ....

Author: ....

Materials: ....

....

....

....

Preparation Needed: ....

....

....

....

Lesson: .... **Time Needed:** ....

....

....

....

....

....

....

Important Reference Pages: ....

....

....

....

Trait Connections: ....

....

....

....

Additional Comments: ....

....

....

Weekly Lesson Plan Form

Teacher: _____   **Week of:** _____

Monday

Trait:	Writing Mode:
_____ Ideas	_____ Descriptive
_____ Organization	_____ Narrative
_____ Voice	_____ Imaginative
_____ Word Choice	_____ Expository
_____ Sentence Fluency	_____ Persuasive
_____ Conventions	
_____ Presentation	

Book: _____

Tuesday

Trait:	Writing Mode:
_____ Ideas	_____ Descriptive
_____ Organization	_____ Narrative
_____ Voice	_____ Imaginative
_____ Word Choice	_____ Expository
_____ Sentence Fluency	_____ Persuasive
_____ Conventions	
_____ Presentation	

Book: _____

Wednesday

Trait:	Writing Mode:
_____ Ideas	_____ Descriptive
_____ Organization	_____ Narrative
_____ Voice	_____ Imaginative
_____ Word Choice	_____ Expository
_____ Sentence Fluency	_____ Persuasive
_____ Conventions	
_____ Presentation	

Book: _____

Thursday

Trait:	Writing Mode:
_____ Ideas	_____ Descriptive
_____ Organization	_____ Narrative
_____ Voice	_____ Imaginative
_____ Word Choice	_____ Expository
_____ Sentence Fluency	_____ Persuasive
_____ Conventions	
_____ Presentation	

Book: _____

Friday

Trait:	Writing Mode:
_____ Ideas	_____ Descriptive
_____ Organization	_____ Narrative
_____ Voice	_____ Imaginative
_____ Word Choice	_____ Expository
_____ Sentence Fluency	_____ Persuasive
_____ Conventions	
_____ Presentation	

Book: _____

Year-Long Writing Assessment Form

Student Name: _____

Grade: _____

Teacher: _____

Assessment Date: _____ Overall Writing Score 1 2 3 4 5

Assessment Date: _____ Overall Writing Score 1 2 3 4 5

Assessment Date: _____ Overall Writing Score 1 2 3 4 5

Assessment Date: _____ Overall Writing Score 1 2 3 4 5

Assessment Date: _____ Overall Writing Score 1 2 3 4 5

Assessment Date: _____ Overall Writing Score 1 2 3 4 5

	1 Experimenting	2 Emerging	3 Developing	4 Effective	5 Strong
Ideas					
Organization					
Voice					
Word Choice					
Sentence Fluency					
Conventions					
Presentation					

PART II

Reproducible Forms for Teaching the Writing Modes

The writing modes—narrative, expository, persuasive, descriptive, and imaginative—provide students with a purpose for writing. The various purposes the modes provide are, respectively, to tell a story, to inform or explain, to construct an argument, to paint a picture with words, or to create a new way of seeing things. By encouraging students to write within these modes, you help them broaden their writing skills by approaching topics with different purposes in mind. They learn to organize their writing for each mode, write to different audiences, and utilize the traits of good writing.

The forms in this section support this kind of instruction. Included are send-home letters to educate and involve parents, checklists to keep students focused on their writing and to help you assess it, and tools to help students organize their thoughts before and as they write within individual modes.

Parent Communication

As students begin writing in the modes, communication between school and home is important to their success. The forms in this section acquaint parents with the language of the writing modes and give them ways to become actively involved in their children's learning.

PARENT LETTER ON MODES

This letter familiarizes parents with the language of the modes. At the beginning of the school year, send a copy home with each student to inform parents of how they can support their children's efforts, whether the assignment calls for a narrative, expository, persuasive, descriptive, or imaginative piece. Or adapt the letter to align more closely with your curriculum requirements and goals.

SEE PAGE 46

ACTIVITIES TO ENCOURAGE WRITING IN THE MODES AT HOME

Parents will appreciate these ideas for encouraging writing at home. By photocopying all of the activities to the back of the parent letter, you supply a useful, one-page menu of options to consider. You might also send home activities periodically to keep fresh ideas flowing throughout the year. Whether they're writing a persuasive piece on a TV show they want to watch, an imaginative piece on the family's next vacation, or an expository piece on rules to a favorite game, students will get plenty of purposeful practice.

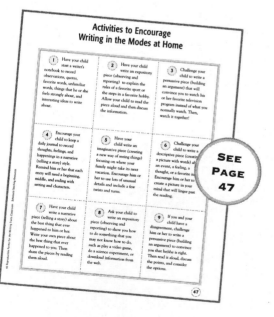

SEE PAGE 47

STUDENT-TO-PARENT LETTERS

The Student-to-Parent Letters define the writing modes for parents and involve them in their child's writing. As you work on each mode, make photocopies of the appropriate letter, distribute them to students, and have students attach the letter to their writing. Each letter encourages the student to read his or her work aloud and then have parents fill in the quick checklist. Students and parents then discuss each checklist statement, which always inspires ideas for revision. Sending these letters home on a regular basis will help parents become more skilled at encouraging improvements in the writing modes.

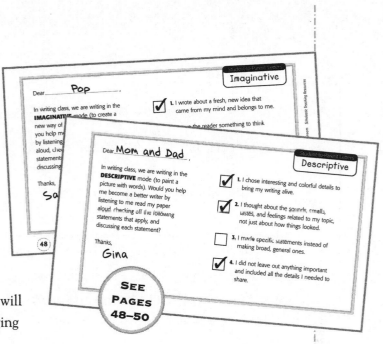

SEE PAGES 48–50

Dear Parent:

As your child becomes familiar with the traits of good writing, he or she will also be learning the modes of writing:

- ◆ Narrative (to tell a story)

- ◆ Expository (to inform or explain)

- ◆ Persuasive (to construct an argument)

- ◆ Descriptive (to paint a picture with words)

- ◆ Imaginative (to create a new way of seeing things)

By writing within these modes, students learn to clarify the purpose for writing, choose the appropriate organization, write to the desired audience, and utilize the traits of good writing.

As students work on each mode throughout the year, I'd like to request your help. Periodically, your child will come home with a mode-specific Student-to-Parent Letter that contains a checklist. He or she will ask you to listen, read a piece of writing aloud to you, and then have you review the piece using the checklist. By providing a good listening ear and a few minutes of constructive discussion, you can help your child see that writing is purposeful, creative, and fun! Thank you for your help.

Sincerely,

40 Reproducible Forms for the Writing Traits Classroom   Scholastic Teaching Resources

Activities to Encourage
Writing in the Modes at Home

1 Have your child start a writer's notebook to record observations, quotes, favorite words, unfamiliar words, things that he or she feels strongly about, and interesting ideas to write about.

2 Have your child write an expository piece (observing and reporting) to explain the rules of a favorite sport or the steps in a favorite hobby. Allow your child to read the piece aloud and then discuss the information.

3 Challenge your child to write a persuasive piece (building an argument) that will convince you to watch his or her favorite television program instead of what you normally watch. Then, watch it together!

4 Encourage your child to keep a daily journal to record thoughts, feelings, and happenings in a narrative (telling a story) style. Remind him or her that each entry will need a beginning, middle, and ending with setting and characters.

5 Have your child write an imaginative piece (creating a new way of seeing things) focusing on where your family might take its next vacation. Encourage him or her to use lots of unusual details and include a few twists and turns.

6 Challenge your child to write a descriptive piece (creating a picture with words) about an event, a feeling, a thought, or a favorite item. Encourage him or her to create a picture in your mind that will linger past the reading.

7 Have your child write a narrative piece (telling a story) about the best thing that ever happened to him or her. Write your own piece about the best thing that ever happened to you. Then share the pieces by reading them aloud.

8 Ask your child to write an expository piece (observing and reporting) to show you how to do something that you may not know how to do, such as play a video game, do a science experiment, or download information from the web.

9 If you and your child have a disagreement, challenge him or her to write a persuasive piece (building an argument) to convince you that he/she is right. Then read it aloud, discuss the points, and consider the options.

Dear _____ ,

In writing class, we are writing in the **DESCRIPTIVE** mode (to paint a picture with words). Would you help me become a better writer by listening to me read my paper aloud, checking off the following statements that apply, and discussing each statement?

Thanks,

☐ **1.** I chose interesting and colorful details to bring my writing alive.

☐ **2.** I thought about the sounds, smells, tastes, and feelings related to my topic, not just about how things looked.

☐ **3.** I made specific statements instead of making broad, general ones.

☐ **4.** I did not leave out anything important and included all the details I needed to share.

Dear _____ ,

In writing class, we are writing in the **IMAGINATIVE** mode (to create a new way of seeing things). Would you help me become a better writer by listening to me read my paper aloud, checking off the following statements that apply, and discussing each statement?

Thanks,

☐ **1.** I wrote about a fresh, new idea that came from my mind and belongs to me.

☐ **2.** I gave the reader something to think about.

☐ **3.** I included lots of colorful and unusual details to get the reader's imagination going.

☐ **4.** I incorporated some interesting twists and turns in the plot of my story.

40 Reproducible Forms for the Writing Traits Classroom   Scholastic Teaching Resources

Narrative

Dear_____ ,

In writing class, we are writing in the **NARRATIVE** mode (to tell a story). Would you help me become a better writer by listening to me read my paper aloud, checking off the following statements that apply, and discussing each statement?

Thanks,

☐ **1.** I let the reader know when and where the story takes place.

☐ **2.** I made my characters seem authentic, with real feelings and thoughts; gave them interesting things to say; and showed them doing things they like to do or don't like to do.

☐ **3.** I told things in an order that makes sense and keeps the reader wanting to know what will happen next.

☐ **4.** I ended my story in a good spot by showing how everything turned out, without going on for too long.

- -

Expository

Dear_____ ,

In writing class, we are writing in the **EXPOSITORY** mode (to inform or explain). Would you help me become a better writer by listening to me read my paper aloud, checking off the following statements that apply, and discussing each statement?

Thanks,

☐ **1.** I tried to teach my reader something he or she didn't already know.

☐ **2.** I used creative and interesting examples to support my writing.

☐ **3.** I thought of questions the reader might ask and tried to answer them.

☐ **4.** I made everything clear and easy to understand.

Persuasive

Dear_____,

In writing class, we are writing in the **PERSUASIVE** mode (to construct an argument). Would you help me become a better writer by listening to me read my paper aloud, checking off the following statements that apply, and discussing each statement?

Thanks,

☐ **1.** I made my position very clear to the reader.

☐ **2.** I chose one position and stuck with it throughout the writing.

☐ **3.** I provided the reader with good, sound reasons for agreeing with my position.

☐ **4.** I considered the other side of the argument and explained its weaknesses to the reader.

Writing Process

Dear_____,

In writing class, we use the **writing process** to go from ideas to published papers. Whether I'm writing at home or at school, I will follow these steps.

Hope you enjoy reading my paper.

1. **Prewrite:** Brainstorm ideas, narrow topic, define purpose and audience

2. **Rough Draft:** Get ideas down on paper

3. **Read Aloud:** Make sure the message makes sense and is easy to read aloud

4. **Writing Groups:** Get feedback, tell back main ideas, praise what works well, ask questions

5. **Revise:** Fine-tune ideas, check organization, consider voice, check word choice, review sentence fluency

6. **Edit:** Double check conventions

7. **Final Copy:** Polish the presentation

8. **Publish and Share:** You are a writer!

Checklists

Checklists are a quick and easy way for you and your students to identify strengths and weaknesses in pieces of writing. As you check off statements, students learn how closely their papers meet the criteria for each mode. Then you can use this information to discuss revision possibilities.

QUICK CHECKS FOR STUDENTS

These forms allow students to think about the criteria for each mode before, during, and after writing. Just choose the appropriate Quick Check for the mode in which students are writing and have them fill it out as a prewriting activity. Once students have drafted their pieces, ask them to review their writing against the checklist statements once more before publishing. Then have students attach the completed checklists to their pieces and refer to them in conferences.

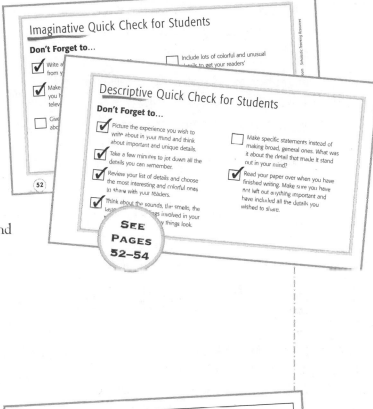

PAPER CLIPPERS

Paper Clippers help you raise students' awareness of strong and weak areas in their writing. They also help you show connections between the traits of writing and the modes of writing. Photocopy and cut out as many as you need. Then assess individual student papers according to the criteria on each form and clip forms to the papers for students to review.

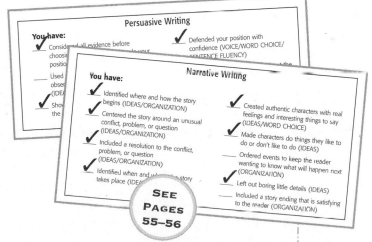

Descriptive Quick Check for Students

Don't Forget to...

☐ Picture the experience you wish to write about in your mind and think about important and unique details.

☐ Take a few minutes to jot down all the details you can remember.

☐ Review your list of details and choose the most interesting and colorful ones to share with your readers.

☐ Think about the sounds, the smells, the tastes, and the feelings involved in your topic, not just about how things look.

☐ Make specific statements instead of making broad, general ones. What was it about the detail that made it stand out in your mind?

☐ Read your paper over when you have finished writing. Make sure you have not left out anything important and have included all the details you wished to share.

Imaginative Quick Check for Students

Don't Forget to...

☐ Write about a fresh idea that comes from your mind and belongs to you.

☐ Make your story different from things you have read in books or seen on television or in the movies.

☐ Give your reader something to wonder about.

☐ Include lots of colorful and unusual details to get your readers' imaginations going.

☐ Incorporate some interesting twists and turns in the plot of your story.

☐ Include creative details that no one else would think of.

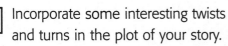

Narrative Quick Check for Students

Don't Forget to...

- ☐ Think about where and how your story begins.
- ☐ Create an opening for your story that makes the reader want to keep reading.
- ☐ Center your story around an unusual conflict, problem, or question.
- ☐ Figure out how the conflict, problem, or question will be resolved.
- ☐ Let the readers know when and where the story takes place.
- ☐ Make your characters seem authentic, with real feelings and thoughts.

- ☐ Give your characters interesting things to say.
- ☐ Show your characters doing things they like to do or don't like to do.
- ☐ Tell things in an order that makes sense and keeps the reader wanting to know what will happen next.
- ☐ Skip over or leave out boring little details that do not matter to the story.
- ☐ Tell readers everything they need to know to get the point of your story.
- ☐ End your story in a good spot by showing how everything turned out, without going on for too long.

Expository Quick Check for Students

Don't Forget to...

- ☐ Pull together enough information to write confidently on your topic.
- ☐ Search for hidden and unusual details that most people wouldn't know.
- ☐ Try to teach your readers something they didn't know.
- ☐ Make everything clear and easy to understand.
- ☐ Spend extra time and care with the most important parts of your writing.

- ☐ Be sure to explain any unusual words, phrases, or terms.
- ☐ Use creative and interesting examples to support your writing.
- ☐ Include a brief history of your topic if it would help stress a point or make things clearer.
- ☐ Think of what questions readers might ask themselves and try to answer them.

Persuasive Quick Check for Students

Don't Forget to...

☐ Consider all evidence before making up your mind about your position on the topic.

☐ Make your position very clear to readers.

☐ Use researched facts, good examples, and observations to make your argument strong.

☐ Consider what the other side of the argument might have to say.

☐ Defend your position with wit, humor, and confidence.

☐ Choose one position and stick with it throughout the writing.

☐ Provide readers with good, sound reasons for agreeing with your position.

☐ Avoid sounding angry or sarcastic in your argument.

☐ Show readers the weaknesses in the opposing viewpoint.

- -

The Writing Process Quick Check for Students

☐ **1. Prewrite**
Brainstorm ideas
Narrow topic
Define purpose and audience

☐ **2. Rough Draft**
Get ideas down on paper

☐ **3. Read Aloud**
Make sure the message makes sense and it is easy to read aloud

☐ **4. Writing Groups**
Get feedback
Tell back main ideas
Praise what works well
Ask questions

☐ **5. Revise**
Fine-tune ideas
Check organization
Consider voice
Check word choice
Review sentence fluency

☐ **6. Edit**
Double check conventions

☐ **7. Final Copy**
Polish the presentation

☐ **8. Publish and Share**
You are a writer!

40 Reproducible Forms for the Writing Traits Classroom *Scholastic Teaching Resources*

Paper Clippers

Descriptive Writing

You have:

_____ Captured experiences and formed pictures with words (IDEAS/WORD CHOICE)

_____ Included good details (IDEAS/WORD CHOICE)

_____ Chosen the most interesting details (IDEAS)

_____ Included sounds, smells, tastes, and feelings (IDEAS/WORD CHOICE)

_____ Included statements specific to topic (IDEAS/WORD CHOICE)

_____ Reread to identify missing information or details (IDEAS/SENTENCE FLUENCY/ORGANIZATION)

Persuasive Writing

You have:

_____ Considered all evidence before choosing your position and made your position clear to readers (IDEAS)

_____ Used researched facts, examples, and observations for a strong argument (IDEAS/ORGANIZATION)

_____ Shown evidence that the other side of the argument was considered (IDEAS)

_____ Defended your position with confidence (VOICE/WORD CHOICE/SENTENCE FLUENCY)

_____ Stuck with one position throughout the writing and provided readers with good, sound reasons to agree (IDEAS/WORD CHOICE)

_____ Shown readers the weaknesses in the opposing viewpoint (IDEAS)

Imaginative Writing

You have:

_____ Employed original and new ideas (IDEAS)

_____ Utilized original ideas not found in books, television, or movies (IDEAS)

_____ Given readers something to wonder about (IDEAS)

_____ Included colorful and unusual details (IDEAS/WORD CHOICE)

_____ Included interesting twists and turns (IDEAS/ORGANIZATION)

_____ Included creative or unique details (IDEAS/WORD CHOICE)

Scholastic Teaching Resources

40 Reproducible Forms for the Writing Traits Classroom

Paper Clippers

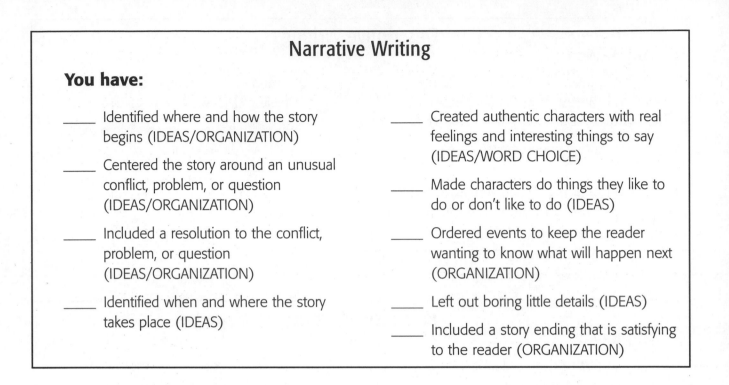

Narrative Writing

You have:

_____ Identified where and how the story begins (IDEAS/ORGANIZATION)

_____ Centered the story around an unusual conflict, problem, or question (IDEAS/ORGANIZATION)

_____ Included a resolution to the conflict, problem, or question (IDEAS/ORGANIZATION)

_____ Identified when and where the story takes place (IDEAS)

_____ Created authentic characters with real feelings and interesting things to say (IDEAS/WORD CHOICE)

_____ Made characters do things they like to do or don't like to do (IDEAS)

_____ Ordered events to keep the reader wanting to know what will happen next (ORGANIZATION)

_____ Left out boring little details (IDEAS)

_____ Included a story ending that is satisfying to the reader (ORGANIZATION)

Expository Writing

You have:

_____ Gathered enough information to show confidence in your topic (IDEAS)

_____ Included interesting and unusual details (IDEA/WORD CHOICE)

_____ Told readers something they may not know (IDEAS)

_____ Written in a clear and easy-to-understand way (IDEAS/WORD CHOICE/SENTENCE FLUENCY)

_____ Spent extra time and care on the most important parts (IDEAS/ORGANIZATION)

_____ Explained unusual words, phrases, or terms (WORD CHOICE)

_____ Included creative and interesting supporting examples (IDEAS/VOICE)

_____ Included maps, charts, graphs, tables, or illustrations when appropriate (PRESENTATION/IDEAS)

_____ Included a brief history of the topic if necessary (IDEAS)

_____ Anticipated and answered the readers' questions (IDEAS)

40 Reproducible Forms for the Writing Traits Classroom   Scholastic Teaching Resources

Quick References and Graphic Organizers

To write well in any mode, students need tools to help them understand the purpose for the writing and organize their thoughts. The reference sheets and graphic organizers in this section provide those tools. They help students focus on what their writing needs in order to become powerful.

SEE PAGE 58

SEE PAGES 59–63

SEE PAGE 64

WRITING MODES QUICK REFERENCE

The Writing Modes Quick Reference is a useful form to photocopy and place in students' writing notebooks to remind them, at a glance, of each mode's definition and characteristics. Encourage students to use it as a review tool before they write, and as an at-home reference while they write with their parents.

"LET'S PICTURE WRITING" GRAPHIC ORGANIZERS

These graphic organizers help students think through their purpose for writing and record ideas, details, sentences, and words before they begin drafting. Photocopy the organizer for the mode in which students are writing to help them determine their direction. Once students have finished writing, have them use their filled-out organizers to make sure they have addressed everything they wanted to write, in the sequence they wished to present it.

EDITOR'S MARKS REFERENCE SHEET

This handy reference sheet acquaints young writers with common editor's marks. Photocopy enough for the class and encourage students to use the sheets when they're editing their papers for style and accuracy.

Writing Modes Quick Reference

Descriptive Writing

Descriptive writing creates a vivid image in the reader's mind and uses "just right" words and phrases to make a "visual picture" linger beyond the reading. Some examples of descriptive pieces are:

menus   travel brochures   catalogs   letters   journals

Narrative Writing

Narrative writing recounts a personal experience or original story. It always includes characters, a setting, and a plot. Some examples of narrative pieces are:

novels   short stories   journals   diaries   autobiographies

Imaginative Writing

Imaginative writing ventures beyond the known and into new territory. The writer plays with creative, original ideas to bring the reader into a new world. Some examples of imaginative pieces are:

tall tales   fables   fairy tales   science fiction   mysteries

Expository Writing

Expository writing is meant to inform, explain, clarify or define, but it often entertains as well. The reader should learn something new and feel that the writer is knowledgeable on the topic. This genre includes expository reports, recounts, explanations, and procedures. Some examples of expository pieces are:

essays   resumes   instructions   directions   research papers

Persuasive Writing

Persuasive writing is used to influence the reader's thinking by crafting an argument using logic, wit, winning language, and skillfully-presented evidence. Some examples of persuasive pieces are:

editorials   advertisements   movie reviews   restaurant critiques

40 Reproducible Forms for the Writing Traits Classroom   Scholastic Teaching Resources

Let's Picture Narrative Writing: To Tell a Story

Name: _____

Piece: _____

Date: _____

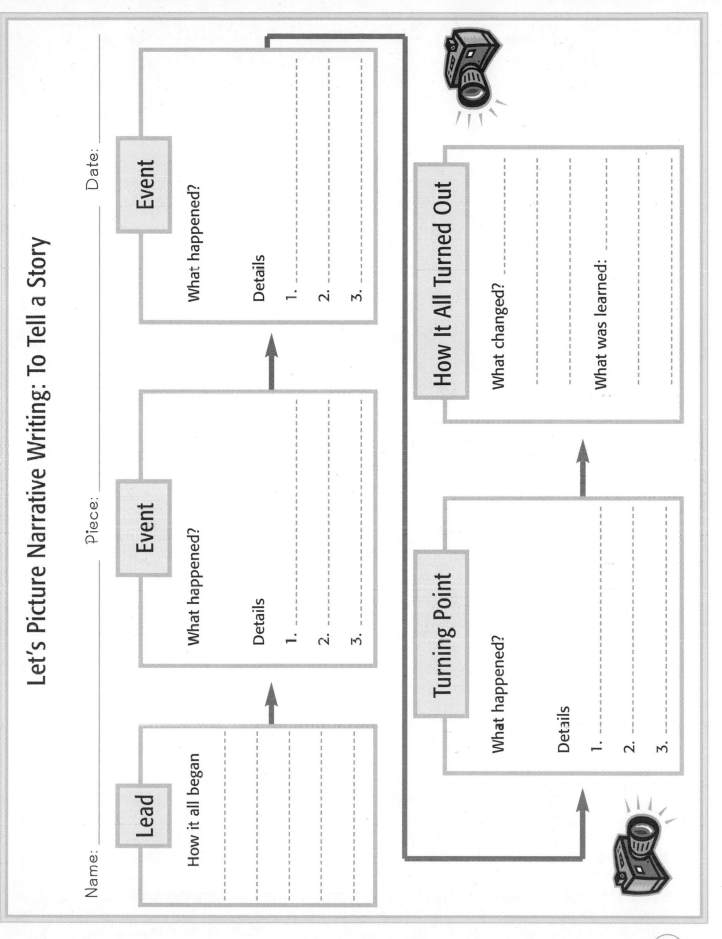

Lead

How it all began

_____

_____

_____

_____

Event

What happened?

_____

Details

1. _____

2. _____

3. _____

Event

What happened?

_____

Details

1. _____

2. _____

3. _____

Turning Point

What happened?

_____

Details

1. _____

2. _____

3. _____

How It All Turned Out

What changed? _____

_____

_____

What was learned: _____

_____

Let's Picture Expository Writing: To Inform or Explain

Name: _____

Piece: _____

Date: _____

The first thing I want to tell you is:

- - - - - - - - - - - - - - - - -
- - - - - - - - - - - - - - - - -
- - - - - - - - - - - - - - - - -

Details: - - - - - - - - - - - - -
- - - - - - - - - - - - - - - - -
- - - - - - - - - - - - - - - - -

Another thing you might find interesting:

- - - - - - - - - - - - - - - - -
- - - - - - - - - - - - - - - - -

Details: - - - - - - - - - - - - -
- - - - - - - - - - - - - - - - -
- - - - - - - - - - - - - - - - -

Central Idea

- - - - - - - - - - - - - - - - -
- - - - - - - - - - - - - - - - -
- - - - - - - - - - - - - - - - -
- - - - - - - - - - - - - - - - -
- - - - - - - - - - - - - - - - -

I've saved the best for last:

- - - - - - - - - - - - - - - - -
- - - - - - - - - - - - - - - - -
- - - - - - - - - - - - - - - - -

Details: - - - - - - - - - - - - -
- - - - - - - - - - - - - - - - -
- - - - - - - - - - - - - - - - -

One last thought to keep in mind:

- - - - - - - - - - - - - - - - -
- - - - - - - - - - - - - - - - -

Details: - - - - - - - - - - - - -
- - - - - - - - - - - - - - - - -
- - - - - - - - - - - - - - - - -

40 Reproducible Forms for the Writing Traits Classroom   Scholastic Teaching Resources

Let's Picture Persuasive Writing: To Construct an Argument

Name: _____

Piece: _____

Date: _____

My Reasons and Evidence

Reason:

Evidence:

Reason:

Evidence:

Reason:

Evidence:

Strong Finish

After weighing
all the pros and cons...

Pros
and
Cons

Counter Arguments

You could argue that:

But here's the weakness:

Here's what I think:

Main
Idea

Let's Picture Descriptive Writing: To Paint a Picture With Words

Name: _____

Piece: _____

Date: _____

What little details can I share that my reader might not know?

- - - - - - - - - - - -
- - - - - - - - - - - -
- - - - - - - - - - - -
- - - - - - - - - - - -

What are the most important details?

- - - - - - - - - - - -
- - - - - - - - - - - -
- - - - - - - - - - - -

What new pictures can I paint in the reader's mind?

- - - - - - - - - - - -
- - - - - - - - - - - -
- - - - - - - - - - - -

Topic

- - - - - - - - - - - -
- - - - - - - - - - - -

What details about my topic do I picture when I close my eyes?

- - - - - - - - - - - -
- - - - - - - - - - - -
- - - - - - - - - - - -
- - - - - - - - - - - -

What unusual details can I include?

- - - - - - - - - - - -
- - - - - - - - - - - -
- - - - - - - - - - - -
- - - - - - - - - - - -

What sensory details can I include?

- - - - - - - - - - - -
- - - - - - - - - - - -
- - - - - - - - - - - -
- - - - - - - - - - - -

Let's Picture Imaginative Writing: To Create a New Way of Seeing Things

Name: _____

Piece: _____

Date: _____

Voice & Audience

I am writing as: _____

My audience is: _____

Interesting Language

Metaphors: _____

Alliteration: _____

Rhymes: _____

Unusual Details

Unusual details I wish to include: _____

New Idea

I plan to create: _____

Twists & Turns

Surprises for the reader: _____

Editor's Marks

℘	Delete material.	The writing is is good.
(sp)	Correct spelling or spell it out.	We are learning ②traits this (weak.)
∩	Close space.	To day is publishing day.
∧	Insert a letter, word, or phrase.	My teacher has books. wonderful
∧	Change a letter.	She is a great wroter.
#̂	Add a space.	Don't forget agood introduction.
∼	Transpose letters or words.	She raed the piece with flair!
≡	Change to a capital letter.	We have j.k. Rowling to thank for Harry Potter's magic.
/	Change to a lowercase letter.	The "Proof is in the Pudding" was his favorite saying.
¶	Start a new paragraph.	"What day is it?" he inquired. "It's Christmas," returned Tiny Tim.
⊙	Add a period.	Use all the traits as you write

40 Reproducible Forms for the Writing Traits Classroom   Scholastic Teaching Resources